CW00823511

A BOOT UP

THE NORTHUMBERLAND
NATIONAL PARK

Anthony Toole

First published in Great Britain in 2011

British Library Cataloguing-in-Publication Data
A CIP record for this title is available from the British Library

ISBN 978 0 85710 034 4

PiXZ Books
Halsgrove House, Ryelands Industrial Estate,
Bagley Road, Wellington, Somerset TA21 9PZ
Tel: 01823 653777
Fax: 01823 216796
email: sales@halsgrove.com

An imprint of Halstar Ltd, part of the Halsgrove group of companies
Information on all Halsgrove titles is available at: www.halsgrove.com

Printed and bound in China by Toppan Leefung Printing Ltd

Contents

The Northumberland National Park

How to use this book

The Area

The Northumberland National Park is long and narrow. It begins near the Scottish Border, to which it clings for almost half its length, and snakes southward to the earlier border marked by Hadrian's Wall. In its length, of approximately 45 miles (72 kilometres), it passes through several geological zones, each of which gives rise to its own landforms, vegetation and scenery.

Oldest are the volcanic rocks of the Cheviot Hills. Formed around 380 million years ago, these rounded, grassy summits once rose above 15000 feet (4500 metres), but have since been ground down by relentless weathering to one-sixth of their early prominences. Shallow seas eroded their bases and laid down mud, shales and sandstone sediments that date back 340 million years.

Following this era, a vast river delta deposited the coarse-grained particles that hardened into the fell sandstones that characterise the heather-clad hills of central Northumberland. The carboniferous era of 300 million years ago saw the deposition of the limestone and coal that would bring wealth to Britain during the modern age. Toward the end of the Carboniferous, more volcanic upheavals forced the dolerite of the Great Whin Sill through the lime-stones to create the crags that now line the southern boundary of the National Park. All this geology was given its final sheen by the Ice Age glaciers that overlapped the history of modern humans.

In the most unlikely of places are rocks carved with the secret graffiti of the Stone Age. These have been superceded by the burial mounds and hill forts of the Bronze and Iron Ages. The Romans left their mark in the roads and forts that extended far to the north of Hadrian's Wall. Castles and fortified dwellings recall the five centuries of border conflict that followed the Norman Conquest, while the relics of the Industrial Revolution can be seen in the abandoned mine workings and spoil heaps that dot the area.

Yet the legacy of this remarkable history is one of the most stunningly beautiful regions of Britain, high, wild and lonely, where the sky is wide and the weather fickle, where the loudest sounds are likely to be the hiss of wind, the babble of water and the distant calls of skylark, lapwing and curlew.

The Routes

Northumberland is an empty county, and the National Park encompasses the more remote regions, up to and including the Pennines. Indeed, the Pennine Way long distance footpath is a recurrent theme throughout these walks. Most follow public rights-of-way, and are suitable for families,

though some tracks become indistinct in places, and a few walks stray for short distances away from tracks. They generally cross high, open moorland, where the weather can change quickly, and boggy ground is often encountered. Strong walking boots are essential, and waterproof/windproof clothing should be carried.

Starting points are given as Ordnance Survey grid references. Directions specify compass points as follows: N (north), NNE (north-northeast), NE (northeast), ENE (east-northeast), E (east), ESE (east-southeast), SE (southeast), SSE (south-southeast), S (south), SSW (south-southwest), SW (southwest), WSW (west-southwest), W (west), WNW (west-northwest), NW (north-west) and NNW (north-northwest).

The remoteness of the walks means that, on the majority, one is unlikely to meet anyone else. The disadvantage is that, with the single exception of the southernmost, the starts are not served by public transport.

The Maps

The route maps in the book should be regarded as only rough guides. Good, detailed maps are essential, as are the skills in using them, and a compass should also be carried. Different parts of the National Park are covered by Ordnance Survey maps in the Landranger series: 74 (Kelso and Coldstream), 80 (Cheviot Hills and Kielder Water), 81 (Alnwick and Morpeth) and 87 (Hexham and Haltwhistle).

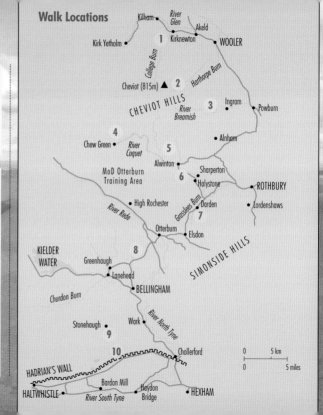

Key to Symbols Used

Level of difficulty:

Easy 🐾

Fair 🐾 🐾

More challenging 🐾 🐾 🐾

Map symbols:

🚗   Park & start

——   Road

-----   Footpath

■   Building / Town

+   Church

🍺   Pub

✺   Settlement or fort

O   Cairn

Walk Locations

Kilham

River Glen

Akeld

Kirk Yetholm

1

Kirknewton

WOOLER

College Burn

Harthorpe Burn

Cheviot (815m) ▲   **2**

CHEVIOT HILLS

River Breamish

3   Ingram

Powburn

4

Chew Green

River Coquet

5

Alnham

Alwinton

Sharperton

6

Halystone

ROTHBURY

MoD Otterburn Training Area

Grasslees Burn

Darden

Lordenshaws

River Rede

High Rochester

7

Otterburn

Elsdon

KIELDER WATER

8

SIMONSIDE HILLS

Greenhaugh

Lanehead

BELLINGHAM

Churdon Burn

Stonehaugh

Wark

River North Tyne

9

Chollerford

0   5 km

0   5 miles

10

HADRIAN'S WALL

Bardon Mill

HALTWHISTLE

River South Tyne

Haydon Bridge

HEXHAM

Great Hetha

A pleasant 3½-mile walk leading to one of the largest and most wonderfully situated Iron Age hill forts in Northumberland.

College Burn rises out of the sodden peat of the Cheviot summit bog, cascades through the Hen Hole, arguably Northumberland's most dramatic set piece, then runs north to the limit of the National Park. It is the least accessible valley in the county, and one of the most peaceful, its tranquillity being aided by the fact that it is privately owned, and a limited number of cars each day are allowed to drive along it only with prior permission. Yet it hides a rich history, as seen in the numerous forts and settlements that reach from the Bronze and Iron Ages, through the

Level: 🥾 🥾
Length: 3½ miles
Terrain: Surfaced road and grassy hill footpath.
Park and Start: Car park just south of Hethpool, 2 miles south of the B6351 Wooler-Kirk Yetholm road.
Start ref.: NT 894280
Websites: www.college-valley.co.uk

Anglo-Saxon and mediaeval to the present day.

Cheviot ewe and lamb, Elsdon Burn.

1 Turn right (NNE) out of the car park and walk back 300 metres into Hethpool. Continue along the road for a further 300 metres, past the College Valley Estate offices, to a sharp right turn in the road.

Cheviot sheep at Hethpool.

2 Go left (W) over a cattle grid onto the road and follow this for 1100 metres. The hillside on the right has two small plantations and several large areas of gorse. The road snakes around, following the contour

of the valley floor and the northern bank of Elsdon Burn. This part of the walk coincides with a short section of the St Cuthbert's Way long distance footpath.

Elsdon Burn valley.

3 At a fork in the road, part company with St Cuthbert's Way, which takes the right fork, crossing the Scottish Border 2 kilometres farther, then following the Pennine

Hetha Burn valley.

The hillside above the road out of Hethpool, above Elsdon Burn, is marked by lynchets, walled terraces, now grass-covered, that provided level patches for crop cultivation during Anglo-Saxon times.

Way for another 3 kilometres to its starting (or finishing) point at Kirk Yetholm.The left fork brings you SSW, over a cattle grid, along the valley of Hetha Burn, and past a conifer forest on your right. To the left, beside a sheep pen, are the grassy mounds that mark the site of a Bronze or Iron Age settlement, while the outline of a large circular establishment can be seen surrounded by the stumps of a now felled forest.

4 The road swings SE, crossing a bridge over Hetha Burn, and climbs steadily to a gate on a saddle between this valley and that of Trowupburn. 100 metres beyond the gate is a small quarry and a wooden signpost indicating the track up Great Hetha.

5 Follow the track (NE) over a stile and past a small group of mature trees. The track zig-zags up

Trowupburn from Great Hetha.

The Cheviot from the boundary wall of Great Hetha hill fort.

Harrowbog, along the eastern bank of the College Burn, east of Great Hetha, is the largest area of semi-natural woodland in the Northumberland National Park. The woodland fringes and areas of scrub provide a home for a small, isolated, though steadily growing population of rare black grouse.

the hillside, and leads first to a shoulder, marked by a wooden post, then continues upwards, crossing the walls of the hill fort that encircles the entire summit of Great Hetha. The views from here are stunning, and encompass Hethpool to the north-east, Trowupburn valley to the south-west and almost the whole of the College valley to the south, dominated by the broad plateau of the Cheviot. Above the western slopes of College valley is

The Cheviot and College valley from Great Hetha.

Blackhaggs Rigg, and peering over this is the Schill, said by some to offer the finest view on the whole of the Pennine Way.

6 From the northern limit of the hill fort, move off to the north-east, and descend for 200 metres to where a stone wall runs to the western end of a conifer forest.

During the nineteenth century, the estate was owned by Lord Cuthbert Collingwood, who led the British fleet into battle at Trafalgar. He planted acorns in the valley, hoping to ensure that Britain would never be short of oak for the hulls of her navy's ships.

Hethpool from Great Hetha.

College valley.

Turn right (SE) and follow the track along the side of the forest, downhill to reach the main valley road.

7 Turn left (NNE) and follow the road for 600 metres, back to the car park.

2 **The Cheviot**

A demanding 8½-mile hill walk over the summit of Northumberland's highest mountain.

The rounded summit of the Cheviot, visible, and unmistakeable from almost any place in Northumberland, is the shrunken remnant of the once many times taller volcano that spilled its magma here some 380 million years ago. The granite bedrock of the summit is buried beneath peat, sometimes to a depth of metres. On the flanks, it is exposed as rubble fields, and most impressively as tall crags in the northern and eastern clefts of The Bizzle and The Henhole. It is the highest mountain in Northumberland and lies a hard mile

Level: 🌸 🌸 🌸
Length: 8½ miles
Terrain: Surfaced road, grassy hill tracks and slab footpath.
Park and Start: Grassy car parking area half-a-mile north-east of Langleeford, at the end of a minor road running south out of Wooler.
Start ref.: NT 954225
Websites:
www.northumberlandnationalpark.org.uk

from the Pennine Way footpath, so walkers on that route often need to make the difficult decision whether to include it or not on their expedition.

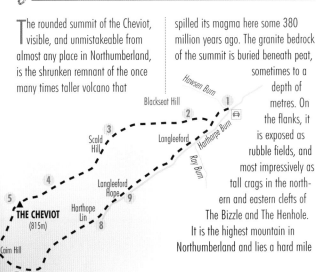

Hawsen Burn
Blackseat Hill
Scald Hill
Langleeford
Harthope Burn
Roy Burn
Langleeford Hope
THE CHEVIOT (815m)
Harthope Lin
Cairn Hill
...sman's Knowe

1 Follow the road (SW) over the bridge toward Langleeford for 300 metres to a break in the small forest on the right. Go through the break and up the rough hillside track, in a generally western direction. After a short distance, the rough gravel gives way to peat. The track undulates for another 300 metres to a gate and stile over a wire fence.

Harthope valley and Hedgehope Hill from the Cheviot.

The Cheviot from Scald Hill.

2 Cross the stile and continue on the track, parallel to the fence. After 600 metres, this leads to a gate at the corner of two fences. Go through this gate and follow the track that runs at a diagonal from the fences. This continues past a series of stone shooting butts. On reaching the next fence, take the track that runs

The stone slabs that constitute the footpath over the Cheviot summit, and several sections of the Pennine Way, came from the floors of demolished Lancashire cotton mills. They were carried to the Cheviot by helicopter.

Stone slabs near Cheviot summit.

left (SW) along this and follow it to a stile at the top of a small rise known as Scald Hill.

(3) Cross the stile and go down the dip and up the slope beyond. This consists of a steady kilo-metre's uphill pull, partly stony, but with a few boggy patches, which eventually levels out at the beginning of a series of stone slabs, and a stile over the fence.

(4) Cross this stile and follow the slabs for 600 metres across level bog to the summit of the Cheviot, marked by a trig point that

The Cheviot is the third highest point on the Pennine chain, its height being exceeded only by those of Cross Fell and Great Dun Fell.

stands on a tall, concrete plinth. Do not step off the slabs, as the ecosys-

Cheviot summit.

tem across the summit plateau is fragile, and the soft, wet peat is, in many places, quite deep.

5 The continuation slabs, away from the summit, belong to a branch linking the top to the Pennine Way footpath. Follow the slabs, crossing a stile after 150 metres, and another, 100 metres farther. A descent of 1100 metres from the Cheviot summit brings you to a wooden signpost on Cairn Hill.

Cheviot summit trig point.

Deep peat on Cheviot summit.

6 Turn left (SSE) and follow the route signposted to Harthope valley and Langleeford, over the stile and steeply downhill, alongside the fence and away from the Pennine Way. Continue down to a stile. Turn left (ESE) and descend into a V-shaped river valley.

7 The river slowly swings round in a leftward curve, eventually moving in a NE direction. Depending on the conditions underfoot, follow the footpath along the riverbank or the parallel alternative that crosses the northern slopes. There are numerous cataracts along the river, and where the valley begins to level out, a wooded gorge with two small, stepped waterfalls. A few hundred metres beyond this is a second gorge, with the waterfall and deep pool of Harthope Linn.

The Cheviot gives its name to a hardy breed of sheep that have roamed these hills since the end of the fourteenth century. Cheviot sheep have been exported to form the breeding nuclei of flocks in Australia and the USA.

Descent to Harthope Burn.

Upper reaches of Harthope Burn.

Harthope Linn.

9 The road now becomes more pronounced, and after 2 kilometres, reaches the farm of Langleeford. A further 750 metres brings you back to the car park.

8 The footpath continues extremely pleasantly for 700 metres beyond Harthope Linn, before passing a set of sheep enclosures, and entering a patch of woodland that opens onto the buildings of Langleeford Hope.

Langleeford.

3 **Dunmoor Hill and Linhope Spout**

A 6½-mile hill walk that descends pleasantly to one of Northumberland's most picturesque waterfalls.

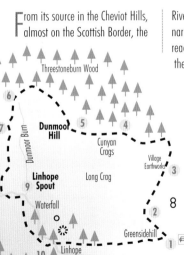

From its source in the Cheviot Hills, almost on the Scottish Border, the River Breamish runs east, through a narrow, steep-sided valley. On reaching the plains, it swings north, then north-west, changes its name to the Till, and becomes a tributary of the Tweed. Scattered around the valley is a high concentration of settlements and hill forts that date back to the Bronze and Iron Ages. The valley road ends at Linhope, though cars cannot progress beyond Hartside. Linhope Burn is a tributary of the

Level: 🥾 🥾 🥾
Length: 6½ miles
Terrain: Rough mountain tracks, sometimes muddy.
Park and Start: Turn west off the A697 a mile north of Powburn. Follow the minor road through Ingram village and for a further 2 miles, to Greensidehill.
Start ref.: NT 984163
Websites:
www.visitnorthumberland.com

Breamish, which joins the main river at Linhope. A kilometre upstream of this is the waterfall of Linhope Spout.

Cross the stile and go uphill (NW) past the house and a marker post. Continue over to the wall and follow this up to and through a gate in a fence, then on to another marker post.

Where the track forks, take the right-hand path (NE), downhill and across boggy ground. The track then rises steadily, crossing a series of wooden footbridges over tiny streams, until it reaches the

Initial slope above Breamish valley.

grassed-over humps and hollows that indicate the site of a Bronze, or Iron Age village. Birds that are commonly seen on this section include lapwing, curlew, raven, buzzard, snipe and skylark.

Go uphill (N) for 300 metres to the corner of the forest,

Remains of Bronze Age village.

Cunyan Crags.

Hedgehope Hill from Dunmoor Hill.

Looking down Linhope Spout.

Linhope Spout waterfall is 60 feet (18 metres) high. Its pool is 6 feet (2 metres) wide and 16 feet (5 metres) deep.

Threestoneburn Wood, then turn left (W) and follow the track along the southern edge of the wood. This rises steadily for 800 metres, swinging round to the north-west, before arriving on the rocky shoulder of Cunyan Crags.

4 The track falls slightly, then rises again, following the fence (W) for 800 metres to a gate at the junction with a second fence running up from the south-west. Go through the gate and across the gentle heathery slope to the summit of Dunmoor Hill. The extensive views from here encompass Hedgehope Hill to the north-west, the Simonside Hills to the south-east and the Northumberland coast to the east.

5 Walk north from the summit boulders to re-join the footpath running alongside the fence. Follow it downhill (NW) for 700 metres to reach a bend in the edge of the wood. Continue along the side of the wood to a stile over a fence, at a sharp bend in the forest.

6 Cross the stile and join a double-wheel track running downhill in a generally south-west direction. Where the track splits, take the right fork, and again at a second split. 200 metres farther, a broad rubble track is reached.

The names of the river, Breamish and Till are Celtic in origin, while those of many of the settlements, such as Ingram and Hartside, demonstrate an Anglo-Saxon influence.

Linhope.

7 Follow this track downhill (S) for a kilometre. It becomes steeper as it approaches the valley. Go through two gates, 100 metres apart, to join a broad, rubble roadway.

8 Turn left (ESE) onto the road, and after 100 metres, cross the bridge over the river. Continue to the top of the rise. Turn left (E) and follow the edge of the slope above the south bank of the river for 200 metres

200 metres north-east of Linhope, just behind the forest and readily accessible by a short ascent from the road, are the ruins of Grieve's Ash, which was the largest Romano-Celtic settlement in Northumberland, covering an area of 20 acres.

to reach Linhope Spout. Descend the steep rocky hillside to the foot of the waterfall. The pool beneath the fall is short and narrow, but deep, and offers the chance of a refreshing bathe on a hot summer's day.

9 Follow the track that leads south, and uphill for 300 metres to a gate in a fence at the

corner of the next small forest. Go through this and on to join a rubble road, which leads, in 400 metres to Linhope village.

10 Go through the village onto the tarred road, which runs east for two kilometres, past Hartside Farm and back to the starting point.

Greenside Hill Farm.

4 Chew Green and Brownhart Law

A 2-mile walk past the ruins of a Roman outpost to the most remote corner of Northumberland.

The Coquet is one of the longest rivers in Northumberland. Second in importance only to the Tyne, it links the towns of Rothbury, Felton, Warkworth and Amble, passing mostly through pleasant agricultural countryside. Upstream of Alwinton, it begins to display a wild face, which grows even wilder as one moves beyond Barrowburn, and past the interlocking ridges that separate its many tributaries. At Chew Green, where the river is born out of the border bogs, the scenery could provide a yardstick for the measurement of bleakness.

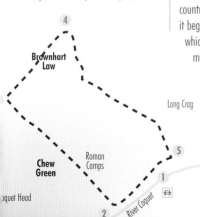

Level: 🥾
Length: 2 miles.
Terrain: Grassy footpaths up gently-sloping hillsides.
Park and Start: About 12 miles along the minor road west of Alwinton, just before the road crosses a bridge over the river onto the MOD land, is a space where several cars may be parked.
Start ref.: NT 794085
Websites:
www.romanbritain.org/places/chew_green.htm
www.otterburnranges.co.uk

Start of walk – bridge leads onto MOD land.

1 Drop down to the bridge. Do not cross it, but walk up the steep, rough track across the road. This brings you, after 250 metres, to a wooden signpost marking a junction with the Pennine Way footpath, which

Signpost, Dere Street.

at this point, coincides with the ancient Roman road, Dere Street.

2 Turn right (NW) and follow Dere Street, which runs along the grassy mounds that indicate the former walls of Chew Green Roman fort. It is worth spending some time exploring the fort. Though it is

Dere Street was one of the most important Roman roads in Britain. Dating from around AD 80, it linked York with Inveresk, on the Firth of Forth in Scotland, passing through the Roman town at Corbridge.

Source of the River Coquet.

Brownhart Law.

grass-covered, the outlines of the walls are easily seen, and enclose a huge area, comparable with that of the much more famous Housesteads

A small herd of shaggy-coated, feral goats patrols back and forth across this stretch of border, and can often be encountered here.

fort, on Hadrian's Wall. Continue directly up the gentle slope beyond the fort, for 300 metres, to reach the wire fence that marks the border with Scotland.

 Turn right (NE) and follow the track alongside the fence.

After 400 metres, this reaches the top of Brownhart Law. The view to the north encompasses an intricate series of hills, cut by deep, steep-sided valleys. Ahead, in the distance, are the summits of the Cheviot and Hedgehope Hill. Continue beyond the top and down to a second fence and gate.

View into Scotland from Brownhart Law.

4 Follow this second fence downhill to the right (S) for 200 metres to regain the Pennine Way footpath. Turn right onto this and follow it for a further 200 metres to a wooden signpost, indicating Chew Green and Makendon. Take the middle of the three tracks that lead away from the signpost, and follow this (SE) over the brow of the hill and down to the road.

5 Turn right and follow the road back to the car park.

Wild goats on the border.

Distant view of the Cheviot from Brownhart Law.

5 Copper Snout and Usway Burn

A 5½-mile walk up a grassy ridge between two narrow valleys, returning along the floor of the deeper valley.

The Upper Coquet valley marks the boundary between the volcanic rocks of the Cheviot Hills to the north and the fell sandstones to the south. In the Coquet Gorge itself, between Alwinton and Linbriggs, the sedimentary shale and limestone layers of the cement-stones are well exposed at Barrow Scar. The northern ramparts of the valley are characterised by a series of grassy ridges that run down from the Scottish Border, and are separated by deep, narrow valleys carved by the many

Level: 🐾 🐾 🐾
Length: 5½ miles.
Terrain: Generally good, and obvious hill tracks and rubble roadways.
Park and Start: Three miles west of Alwinton is Shilmoor Farm. On the south bank of the river, just before the road crosses a bridge, is an area of rough land where cars can be parked.
Start ref.: NT 885077
Websites:
www.northumberlandnationalpark.org.uk

tributaries of the Coquet, of which Usway Burn is the longest.

(1) Cross the bridge and turn right (ESE) to the farm. Go through the gate between the farm buildings and the River Coquet, and cross the bridge over the tributary, Usway Burn. Follow the broad track gently uphill. After 100 metres, this swings sharply to the left and passes a large, well-constructed sheep fold.

In the eighteenth century, several illegal whisky stills were hidden in the Upper Coquet valley. One of these was situated near the upper reaches of Wholehope Burn, below Copper Snout. The whisky sold in the nearby (now demolished) Slymefoot Pub was said to be 'innocent of duty.'

Shillmoor and the River Coquet.

100 metres farther, the track turns right (NNE).

(2) Continue uphill in this line for 1100 metres to reach a gate and stile. The ridge is broad and grassy, but as height is gained, there are opportunities for short detours to enjoy the views to either side, into the deep valleys of Usway Burn to the left, and Wholehope Burn to the right.

Usway Burn and Shillhope Law.

3 Another 1100 metres, almost directly north, brings you to a right turn in the track. A narrower footpath, marked by a wooden post, leads off to the left (NNW). Follow this for 150 metres, where it also turns right (NE) and passes round a small shoulder of the ridge. It continues for a further 600

Wholehope Burn from Copper Snout.

metres in a gently rising curve to a second gate and stile.

Despite the history of border conflict, the name 'Batailshiel Haugh' owes nothing either to battles or shields. It was the site of a thirteenth-century summer farm, or shiel, owned by Henry de Batail. 'Haugh' means 'flat land by a river.'

4 Go over the stile, then turn right (NE), past a sheep fold, and follow the fence for 300 metres to the next gate. The terrain is swampy in a few small areas. The continuation track beyond the gate leads, in 200 metres, to the forest rubble roadway of Clennell Street. The forest that stood on the far side of the road has been recently felled, giving a more open aspect.

Copper Snout.

5 Turn left (NW) and follow Clennell Street for 450 metres to where a signpost indicates a footpath leading off to the left (WNW).

6 The track leads across open moorland for 800 metres, slowly curving to a westerly direction. It then turns south-west and descends the broad ridge for a further 800 metres. Again, there are opportunities for short detours to view the northern and southern mid-sections of Usway Burn.

Usway Burn and corner of Kidland Forest.

Gate and sheep fold, Saughey Hill.

7 The track leads to a fence that runs across a saddle beneath a rounded hill called the Castles. Turn left (SSE) and follow the path alongside the fence. This leads easily downhill over a series of stiles to the buildings of Batailshiel Haugh. The last stile is reached 50 metres before the first farm building, and the last section of footpath runs down onto the rubble road.

Kidland Forest and Windy Gyle.

Valley of Usway Burn.

Batailshiel Haugh.

8 The road runs generally south, for 2.7 kilometres, along the valley floor. As it snakes its way between the steep valley sides, it crosses over three substantial bridges, before arriving at Shillmoor. Turn right at Shillmoor and cross over the bridge to the starting point.

Clennel Street was an old drovers' road linking Morpeth with Kelso, crossing the border about a mile north-east of Windy Gyle. Its Old English name, variously given as Ermspeth (eagle's path), Emspeth and Ernespeth, indicates that it was used more than 1000 years ago.

Bridge, Usway Burn.

6 Harbottle and the Drake Stone

A 2½-mile varied walk through a nature reserve, past one of the most prominent landmarks in Northumberland.

The Harbottle Hills mark the beginning of the more remote reaches of the Upper Coquet valley. The skyline to the west of Harbottle village is dominated by the Drake Stone, a sandstone boulder weighing an estimated 2030 tons. This enormous erratic was carried here by a glacier during the last Ice Age, and there is much additional evidence of glaciation. The hills as far as Harbottle Lake are a nature reserve and Site of Special Scientific Interest, in which mammals such as roe deer and short-tailed voles may be seen, as well as green tiger beetles and brimstone and eggar moths.

Level:
Length: 2½ miles
Terrain: Rough hill and forest tracks, steep and muddy in places.
Park and Start: Car park at eastern corner of wood, 600 metres west of Harbottle village.
Start ref.: NT 926048
Websites:
www.northofthetyne.co.uk/harbottle.html
www.rothbury.co.uk/around/harbottle.htm

Parts of the hillsides have been quarried, and the occasional unfinished and abandoned millstone can be found buried in the heather.

Angryhaugh

West Wood

Harbottle

Drake Stone

Harbottle Wood

Bottle Lake

HARBOTTLE HILLS

1 Follow the rough track alongside the wall that bounds the eastern corner of the forest. After 100 metres, go through the gate into the Harbottle Nature Reserve. Turn right (WSW), past a wooden seat and go up the hillside.

2 200 metres up the hillside is another seat, from which there are good views back to Harbottle village and its ruined castle, and along the Coquet to the Simonside Hills. A further 200 metres beyond this, the track splits. Take the

Harbottle Castle was built in 1160, by Henry II and the Bishop of Durham, on the site of an earlier Saxon fortification. It saw much action during subsequent border conflicts. In 1310, it was captured by Robert the Bruce.

Harbottle Hills and the Drake Stone.

Signpost in car park.

Harbottle village.

left fork, which leads past a third seat and then climbs a little more steeply to a top crowned by a jumble of erratic boulders, the largest of which is the Drake Stone.

3 The track now meanders around the boulders to the north of the Drake Stone, then drops down through deep heather to the shore of Harbottle Lake. Cross the stile

In older texts, the Drake Stone is referred to as the Draag Stone. On its top are carved names and inscriptions that date back to 1805.

Carvings on top of the Drake Stone.

The Drake Stone.

Harbottle Lake and the Drake Stone.

Abandoned millstone near Harbottle Lake.

200 metres to the edge of Harbottle West Wood. Continue in the same direction through the wood, emerging, after 900 metres, onto a broad, rubble roadway.

In 1515, Margaret Tudor, Henry VIII's sister stayed at Harbottle Castle. While there, she gave birth to a daughter, also Margaret, who became grandmother to James VI of Scotland and I of England.

over a fence and continue along the north shore to the second fence, which marks the boundary of the Ministry of Defence Otterburn Ranges. The land that slopes up to the north consists of expanses of glaciated slabs.

 Turn right (N) and follow the track alongside the fence for

Entrance to the forest.

Harbottle Castle.

5 Turn right (NE) and follow the roadway along the northern forest boundary for 800 metres to reach the road. There are good views to the north across the Coquet valley to the village of Alwinton.

6 Turn right (SSE) onto the road and follow it for 600 metres to the car park.

In 1817, Sir Walter Scott stayed at the Rose and Thistle in Alwinton, while writing his novel, Rob Roy.

7 Darden Lough

A 5½-mile hill walk through heather and over grouse moorland to reach two of Northumberland's more remote loughs.

The Simonside Hills, the most easily recognisable in Northumberland, are visible from as far south as County Durham. Simonside itself rises above Rothbury, and was of great spiritual significance to Neolithic and Bronze Age peoples, as seen in the many rock carvings and burial sites scattered around the area. Darden Pike stands at the western end of these hills, and though not visible from Simonside, can be seen to the north-east of Elsdon. A little over a mile north-east of the start of this walk beside the Iron Age fort of Harehaugh Hill, a 5000-year-old burial mound was discovered, which is thought to be the oldest archaeological site in the Coquet valley.

Level: 🥾 🥾
Length: 5½ miles
Terrain: Rough mountain tracks, sometimes muddy.
Park and Start: Car park on the B6341 between Elsdon and Rothbury, 3½ miles from Elsdon.
Start ref.: NY959981
Websites: www.otterburnranges.co.uk
www.visitnorthumberland.com

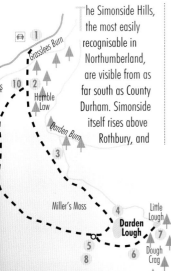

Grasslees Burn

Humble Law

Darden Burn

Miller's Moss

Little Lough

Darden Lough

Dough Crag

7

Darden Lough

① Go through the gate and follow the track downhill to the south, over a tiny stream and on to a broad, wooden bridge over Grasslees Burn. Cross the bridge and climb over the stile beyond. Follow the broad track uphill to the corner of a fence. Continue up alongside the fence for 100 metres to where the track splits.

Sandy Crags.

The first marker post.

② Take the left fork, uphill for a further 200 metres to the top of a rise. The track now drops to the bed of a small river valley. Cross the stream and go on up the slope beyond. The track diverges from the fence for a few hundred metres, but is

While not the highest in the county, Darden Lough and Little Lough are the highest loughs in the National Park, with Little Lough being the higher by 20 metres.

42

well-worn and marked by white-topped, wooden posts. Sandy Crags makes its appearance, dominating the slopes to the east.

 The track narrows, passes through deep heather and

gradually swings round to the south-east. The hill steepens, then eases off for the last kilometre to the shore of Darden Lough.

 Turn right (SW) and follow the path along the shore for

Elsdon is a mediaeval village, with a broad village green and the remains of an eleventh century motte-and-bailey castle and a fifteenth century Pele Tower, which is still used as a residence.

300 metres to the summit cairn and rocky windbreak of Darden Pike. The view to the north and west encompasses the Otterburn Ranges, from which the sounds of gunfire can often

Darden Lough.

Peat at edge of Darden Lough.

Darden Lough from Darden Pike.

Nestling in the valley to the south-west is the village of Elsdon.

(5) If you wish to include a visit to the, so far hidden, Little Lough, go through the gate (E) to the trig point and continue in the same direction for 500 metres, across the low ground to the south of the lough, and up to the summit of Dough Crag. There is no track, and the land could be swampy after prolonged heavy rain.

In 1877, the bones and skulls of more than 1000 soldiers, killed at the Battle of Otterburn, in 1388, were found buried near the churchyard in Elsdon.

Darden Pike summit.

Lichen, Darden Pike.

(6) Little Lough can be seen, 500 metres to the north-east, and may be reached by a track, again swampy in places, that runs alongside the fenced boundary of the now-felled conifer forest.

Little Lough.

(7) Return to the summit of Darden Pike.

(8) Drop down to the west from the cairn to the wooden marker post, and continue following the track. After 500 metres, this begins to swing in a gentle curve round to the north. Approaching the shoulder of the ridge, the track becomes a little indistinct. However, the marker posts are 200 metres apart, and the path improves again after 400 metres.

(9) The path continues to curve round to the right, to a point from which the road and car park become visible. Pass a high deer fence that surrounds a deciduous wood. Just beyond this, the track splits. Take the narrower path to the right, which after 300 metres, joins the route of ascent.

(10) Turn left (N) onto this and follow it back to the car park.

Blackface sheep and Sandy Crags.

8 Troughend Common

A 3½ mile walk that offers a brief taste of high, exposed and trackless moorland.

The Pennine Way footpath rises from its starting point in Kirk Yetholm, to join the western limit of

Troughend Common

the Northumberland National Park above the College valley. It clings to this until south of Byrness. It then crosses the high, wild moorland of Troughend Common to join the eastern boundary, which it continues to follow until it leaves the Park just south of Hadrian's Wall. This middle section of the Park, west of Otterburn, is, at 7 kilometres (4 Miles), the narrowest. About half of this walk does not follow a track, and so should be undertaken in good weather. If the weather should turn bad, then the road is, at its farthest distance, little more than a mile away to the south.

Level: 🐾 🐾
Length: 3½ miles
Terrain: Partly grassy footpath, partly open moorland without tracks.
Park and Start: 1 kilometre WSW of Hareshaw Head farm on the B6320 between Otterburn and Bellingham, where the Pennine Way crosses the road.
Start ref.: NY 841883
Websites:
www.northumberlandnationalpark.org.uk

Red grouse.

47

1. Cross the stile on the north side of the road. There are two diverging tracks. Take the right-hand one (NNE), which is the Pennine Way footpath. This leads past a colliery spoil heap, and follows wooden marker posts across moorland, with a few small steps over streams. After 700 metres, the path crosses a stone bridge at the bottom of a shallow amphitheatre.

2. The track steepens for 100 metres. This is the steepest part of the walk. At the top of the rise, where the track swings to the

Bridge over tributary of Hareshaw Burn.

left, leave it and walk in a north-easterly direction across wild, open moorland. Continue for 1300 metres, through heather and over several drainage channels, which are now

Hareshaw Burn runs south from Troughend Common to join the River North Tyne at Bellingham. It passes over Hareshaw Linn waterfall and through a narrow gorge, which is a Site of Special Scientific Interest.

Mine spoil heap, Hareshaw Head.

being allowed to re-fill with sphagnum moss. The land dips for a short distance, then rises again to a fence running east-west across Great Moor. Follow this to a gate and go through this to the highest point.

There are good views from here, over Redesdale toward Otterburn, and farther north to the Cheviot and Hedgehope Hill. Birds that you might see here include curlew, skylark,

During the nineteenth century, coal from the mines around Hareshaw Head provided fuel for the Hareshaw Ironworks, the ruins of which can be seen on the banks of Hareshaw Burn, just north of Bellingham.

Sphagnum moss.

Otterburn from Great Moor.

meadow pipit, grouse, golden plover and raven.

(3) Return to the gate. Go through this and turn right (W) to follow the fence for 400 metres to where it bends.

Sphagnum bog, between Great Moor and Deer Play.

Lizard, Deer Play.

4 Turn right (N) and continue to follow the fence for 800 metres, through a depression, with a short stretch of wet, sphagnum bog, then on up the slope beyond to the highest point.

The road at Hareshaw Head is the highest point on the Cyclone Challenge, one of the premier cycling events in the UK, which takes place annually in June, attracting competitors from Britain and overseas.

5 Turn left (WSW) and go up the gentle gradient for 300 metres to re-join the Pennine Way footpath at a signpost with a cairn built around its base. This area of moorland has the colourful name, Deer Play.

6 Go south along the Pennine Way, past two partially grassed-over stone circles to a tall

Summit of Deer Play.

Stone shelter, Deer Play.

The fields to the north of Otterburn saw a bloody battle in 1388, between Scots, under the Earl of Douglas, and English, under Henry 'Harry Hotspur' Percy. Douglas was killed and Percy captured. 100 Scots and over 1000 English also died.

visible route across the moor. The letters C, T and H are carved on the south, north and west sides of the pillar, respectively.

wooden marker post. 100 metres to the east of this is a solitary stone pillar, which appears to be in the process of being slowly swallowed by the peat. This is probably a signpost on a much earlier, and now no longer

Stone marker post, Deer Play.

7 Continue along the Pennine Way, which, 1500 metres south of the tall marker post, brings you back to the road.

9 **Bellcrag Flow**

An enjoyable 5-mile walk with few gradients over open moorland, through conifer forest and across an important area of peat bog.

The forest of Kielder and Wark is Britain's largest man-made forest,

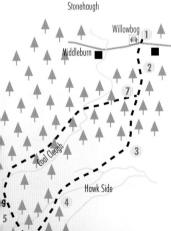

Stonehaugh

and encloses the largest artificial lake in Northern Europe. Scattered throughout the forest, often in fairly inaccessible places, are more than fifty small patches of peat, some little more than a few acres in area, that have never held trees. These are the Border Mires, Sites of Special Scientific Interest, which together constitute a National Nature Reserve. They date from the last Ice Age, and are more than 10 000 years old. They were long regarded as useless tracts of land, but are now known to be globally rare

Level: 🐾 🐾
Length: 5 miles
Terrain: Moorland footpaths and rubble roadways.
Park and Start: Follow the B6320 for about 3½ miles north of Chollerford, until a signpost points a minor road to Stonehaugh. Follow this for 5 miles to where it is crossed by the Pennine Way footpath, about ¾ mile south-east of Stonehaugh.
Start ref.: NY 798752
Websites:
www.northumberlandnationalpark.org.uk/
seeblanketbogs

eco-systems, and among the most important carbon sinks on the planet.

1 Cross the stile and follow the Pennine Way footpath uphill (S), alongside the wire fence. The track levels out after 150 metres, and leads to a second stile at a corner of the forest. A futher 150 metres brings you into the main body of Wark Forest.

Stile and gate between forest and Haughton Common.

2 Follow the Pennine Way sign-posts south through the forest

Bellcrag Flow is a blanket bog, occupying the space once taken up by a shallow lake. It is bounded by two rocky ridges, sandstone to the north and limestone to the south. The peat has an average depth of ten metres.

Start of walk.

Walled enclosure, Haughton Common.

Walkers on the Pennine Way, Haughton Common.

Peat is formed largely from sphagnum mosses, which slowly fill waterlogged areas and on dying, decompose under anaerobic conditions. Its depth increases at a rate of one millimetre each year.

Bellcrag Flow.

for 1100 metres. The track crosses four rubble roadways and a wooden footbridge over a small burn, with a few gentle rises, to reach a gate and stile at the southern boundary of this section of the wood.

(3) Cross the stile onto the open expanse of Haughton Common. Follow the track leading to the right (SW) across the Common. In the distance to the south, are the sandstone rocks of King's Crags and

Pool, Bellcrag Flow.

the Whin Sill dolerite of Sewingshields Crags, over which runs Hadrian's Wall. It is possible, also, to see cars driving along the Military Road. The track passes a small walled enclosure containing trees. Beyond this, it splits. Take the lower, left-hand track. 1.5 kilometres after leaving the forest, the route re-enters it at a stile.

During the 1980s, attempts were made to harvest peat from Bellcrag Flow, but these operations were ended after two years. Now, the bog is being re-generated by the placing of re-cycled plastic piles to block the former drainage channels.

Plastic pile blocking drainage channel.

Sphagnum moss at edge of pool.

 Continue for 500 metres, past two clearings, to a fork in the track. This is where you part company with the Pennine Way footpath. Follow the right fork, signposted to Bellcrag Flow. Go through an area of quarried limestone, and after 250 metres, join a broad rubble roadway. Turn right (NNW) onto this and follow it for 500 metres to the southern edge of Bellcrag Flow.

(5) After spending some time exploring the mire from the

The plants in the mire are ones that can survive in the acid conditions, such as bog asphodel, cranberry and the insect-eating sundew. Insects that thrive here include ten species of dragonfly and damselfly.

(7) Turn left (NNE) onto this path and re-trace your route of the early part of the walk, for 800 metres, back to the starting point.

Lichen on tree.

Forest roadway.

wooden boardwalks, continue along the forest roadway for 300 metres, past the entrance to a sandstone quarry, to the northern edge of Bellcrag Flow.

(6) The roadway curves round toward a north-easterly direction, and after 1.8 kilometres, turns ENE. After a further kilometre, it reaches a junction with the Pennine Way footpath.

10 **Broomlee Lough and the Hidden Loughs**

A very varied and continually interesting 7½-mile walk that passes through three distinct geological zones.

The southern boundary of the Northumberland National Park is overlooked from the north by the central, and most visually impressive section of Hadrian's Wall. Striding along the line of the wall, the walker's attention is continually drawn down to the natural loughs of Crag, Greenlee and Broomlee, nestling in glacial hollows, and beyond to the southern limits of Wark Forest. Hidden among the eskers of Haughton Common, however, are the small, artificial pools of Halleypike Lough and Folly Lake, which were created for fishing during the nineteenth century.

Level: 🥾 🥾 🥾
Length: 7½ miles
Terrain: Grassy footpaths and rough rubble tracks.
Park and Start: Beside the Old Repeater Station, just off the Military Road between Chollerford and Greenhead.
Start ref.: NY 816700
Public transport: Hadrian's Wall Country Bus, AD 122, runs between Carlisle and Newcastle, via Hexham, Haltwhistle and the Military Road, daily from April to October.
Websites: www.hadrians-wall.org
www.northumberlandnationalpark.org.uk

Map labels:
Halleypike Lough
4
6
5
3
King's Crags
7
Hemmel Rigg
Queen's Crags
The Old Repeater Station
2
Sewing Shields
12
Sewingshields Crags
11
enkins Burn
Broomlee Lough
10
Housesteads
VERCOVICIVM ROMAN FORT

Old Repeater Station, Military Road.

1 Go through the gate on the opposite side of the road to the Old Repeater Station, and over the stile on the left. Follow the path (SW) between the wall and fence for 300 metres to a house. Here you will join a rough farm track that curves in a semicircle to the right for 500 metres to Sewingshields Farm. Pass the farm and continue to a single storey house.

2 Turn sharp left (W) and go along the track beneath the wood for 250 metres. The track then turns north for 400 metres, then north-west for a further 500 metres. At the next junction, turn left (NNW), past a limekiln, with a small limestone quarry above and behind it. Continue to a ford, with a wooden bridge thirty metres to the left.

> Repeater Stations made up a network of communications installations, constructed approximately every thirty kilometres, that amplified analogue telephone signals to compensate for energy losses during transmission.

Sewingshields Farm.

Limekilns.

 3 To see the hidden loughs, which cannot be seen from the Roman Wall, cross the bridge and continue to the gate. Go through this and up the slope beyond, to the top of the rise. From here, you will have a good view of the forest-enclosed Folly

Folly Lake and King's Crags.

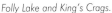

Lake. Continue to the next gate at the bottom of the hill to see Halleypike Lough, which, in complete contrast to its neighbour, is devoid of trees.

4 Return to the bridge.

5 Turn right (W) after re-crossing the bridge, and follow the slope of the glacial esker, converging with the southern boundary of Folly Lake wood. At the western end of the wood, are the grassed-over humps of several Iron Age structures.

So isolated are Halleypike Lough and Folly Lake that they have become sanctuaries for the rare and endangered white-clawed crayfish.

Halleypike Lough and Folly Lake from King's Crags.

Broomlee Lough.

In a northern version of the King Arthur legend, Broomlee Lough is traced as the source, and resting place of Excalibur. King's and Queen's Crags are thought to have been named in honour of Arthur and Guinevere.

 6 Continue in a WSW direction, past a walled enclosure containing a small number of trees, and on up to the top of King's Crags. The

Junction with the Pennine Way.

rock here is of fell sandstone, and there are good views back over the hidden loughs. Continue over the crags and down the slope beyond, until just above the wall that blocks further progress.

7 Drop, down to the left (S) to a gate and stile, and join the broad rubble track on the far side of the wall. Queen's Crags, also of fell sandstone, rises impressively to the left. Follow the track (SW) for 1.5 kilometres, passing through a gate at half way, to a junction with the Pennine Way footpath. Greenlee Lough, the largest natural lake in Northumberland, lies ahead.

Broomlee Lough and Sewingshields Crags.

8 Turn left (S) onto the Pennine Way, and follow this as it curves round to the left and ascends a short slope to a wall. Cross the stile over this and follow the curving track for a further 300 metres to another gate. Broomlee Lough lies to the left, with Sewingshields Crags beyond.

9 Turn left (ENE) onto a track that leads for 1100 metres to a small enclosed wood. Go through this (100 metres) and continue (E) for 400 metres to a stile. Climb over this to join the Hadrian's Wall walk.

10 Turn left (N) and climb the steepening slope for 400 metres to the trig point that marks the summit of Sewingshields Crags.

11 The footpath now turns right (ENE) and follows a section of Hardian's Wall for 750 metres along the top of the Whin Sill, past two turrets and a milecastle, to Sewingshields Wood.

12 Go through the wood, past the farm, to join the route taken earlier, at the single-storey house. Turn right and re-trace the farm track and footpath back to the Old Repeater Station.

Hardrian's Wall and Sewingshields Wood.